CARD GAMES

by

N.A.C. BATHE

CONTENTS

THINGS YOU NEED TO KNOW

THE PACK: a standard pack of cards has 52 cards, divided into 4 suits of 13 cards each. Each suit is clearly marked by its own symbol - Hearts, Clubs, Diamonds and Spades. Each card has a value. Ace is always either top or bottom, depending on the game. Then, from the top, the order is King, Queen, Jack, and the number cards from 10 to 1. There is an extra card, not used in all games, the Joker. Usually you can assign to him any value you want.

SHUFFLING AND CUTTING: at the start of every game, unless the rules say otherwise, the pack is shuffled, so that the cards are thoroughly mixed; and then cut. To cut the pack after it has been shuffled, get another player to lift around half of the shuffled pack, and place that half underneath, so that the upper half of the pack becomes the lower half.

RULES: card games are international, but often there are differences between the American and British versions of a game with the same name. In some cases it's not even the same game. The rules of some games can vary even within the same country. The important thing is to make sure that everyone in the game is playing to the same set of rules.

CUTTING AND DRAWING FOR DEALER: cutting for dealer is letting each player in turn cut the pack to show a card. Drawing is when each player draws a card from the pack. Normally the player with the highest card wins, though in some games it is the lowest. If there is a tie, the players involved try again.

GAMBLING: many card games can be used for gambling. Betting can take many forms: it doesn't have to be money. Currency can be anything from plastic chips to actual cash - whatever you use, don't bet what you haven't got.

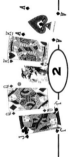

Some card games are very straightforward and others are quite complex. Also, different people pick up rules and techniques at varying speeds. As a very general guide, the games in this book have been given an Easier/Harder rating. A single * indicates Easier, and more **s mean Harder. However, all the games in the book are well within the scope of the average person, even if you have never played before.

TECHNICAL TERMS OF CARD PLAY

Ace High: Ace is top scoring card.

Ace Low: Ace is lowest scoring card.

Ante: Also known as the Stake. The amount each player pays into the Pool at the start of a gambling game.

Available Card: In Patience, a card that can be used in play.

Build Up: In Patience, laying cards in ascending order of value on top of a Foundation Card.

Build Down: Laying the cards in descending order of value.

Chips: Tokens used in gambling games.

Column: Cards laid on the table in an overlapping vertical line.

Court Cards: Kings, Queens and Jacks.

Deal: Passing out cards to players. Most deals are one card at a time to each player, but this can vary according to the game.

Deck: Another word for the Pack.

Discard: In some games, to play a card of no value in the game, when the player cannot follow suit or play a trump. In other games, to play a card to the waste pile.

Eldest Hand: The player on the dealer's left, who normally leads.

File: In Patience, a column in the Layout, with cards overlapping but with suits and pip values visible. Files are built up towards the player.

Flush: A Hand of cards all of the same suit.

Follow Suit: To play a card of the same suit as the first card played in a trick.

Foundation Card: In Patience, a card laid down on which other cards are built up or down. They are normally aces or kings.

Hand: The cards held by a player at any point during the game. In Patience, it can also be any cards which have not been dealt out (also called the Stock).

Honour Cards: Ace, King, Queen and Jack of the trump suit.

Layout: The arrangement of cards in Patience games. Also called the Tableau.

Kitty: See Pool.

Lead: Being first player to set down a card. Also the card played first (lead card).

Meld: A set of three or more of a kind: e.g. either all Kings, or all Hearts (but these must be in sequence of pip value with no gaps).

Number Card: Card of any value between 10 and 2.

Pack: The full set of 52 cards (or 53 with a Joker). Also known as a Deck.

Packet: Set of cards that is less than a full Pack.

Pair: Two cards of the same kind, e.g. two 2's.

Pass: To miss a turn.

Pip Value: The number on a Number Card (e.g. a 9 has nine pips).

Pool: Total amount of cash or gambling chips staked in a game, usually placed in the middle of the table. Also called the kitty, or the pot.

Plain card: Card not of the trump suit.

Play: To play a card is to take it from your hand and use it in the game.

Rank: The value of a card.

Re-deal: In Patience, using the cards from the Waste Pile to deal again, when the Stock is used up.

Renege: To fail to follow suit in a game where following suit is not obligatory. Often confused with Revoke. See Revoke.

Revoke: To play an incorrect card, normally by failing to follow suit when able to; in a game when following suit is obligatory if you can do so. Often confused with Renege.

Round: This is complete once each player has played his cards in any trick.

Row: In Patience, a line of cards placed side by side (suit and pip value must always be visible if cards overlap).

Rubber: A set of games, especially in whist.

Ruff: A trump card. To ruff is to play a trump to a non-trump lead.

School: A group of players playing for money, especially in Poker.

Sequence: The order in which the cards run, from high to low, or the other way round.

Singleton: A single card of any suit.

Stock: The cards remaining after dealing, sometimes also called the Hand.

Tableau: Another word for Layout.

Talon: Another word for Waste Pile.

Trick: The cards played by all the players in a Round, one from each.

Trumps: Cards of a chosen suit that outrank all cards in all other suits during the game. Trumping is playing a trump card.

Waste Pile: Cards turned up in the course of playing Patience that are not available for play according to the rules of the game. Also sometimes called the Talon.

Wild Card: A card which a player can use to represent any other card (within the rules of the game).

PATIENCE

These one-player games are all forms of Patience, also called Solitaire. You need a good-sized table to lay the cards out, though it is possible to find special Patience packs in a smaller size (these can also be useful for other card games when travelling).

ACCORDION *

The Aim: To be left with all the cards in one pile.

The Method: Use the standard 52-card pack. Deal out all the cards, face-up, in a single row, not overlapping. You can then move cards as follows:

Move a card on to the card on its left, if it is the same suit, or the same pip value. Move a card on to the card third from the left, if it is the same suit or the same pip value. After making a move, look to see if additional moves are now possible. When cards are stacked, don't just move the topmost card, but the whole stack, according to the value or suit of the topmost card.

ACES UP **

The Aim: To be left with only the four Aces.

The Method: Use the standard 52-card pack. Cards rank in descending order from Ace to 2. Deal four cards in a row, face-up. If two or more cards of the same suit are dealt, discard the low or lower ones, leaving a space. Deal a further four cards face-up on top of the first ones, including the space(s). Again discard the lower cards of a duplicated suit. An eliminated card may uncover another that can also be eliminated. Once six deals have been made, you can move the top card or cards of any pile into a space, before the next deal. The aim is to discard all cards except the four Aces, and you finish with a row of four Aces.

Note: If a discard is at the top of a pile, only the top card is discarded.

MADE IN BELGIUM

BELEAGUERED CASTLE ***

The Aim: To build up four piles in suit and sequence, Ace (low) to King.

The Method: Use the standard 52-card pack. Take out the four Aces and arrange them in a column (not overlapping). These are your foundation cards. The tableau is made by dealing six cards to each side of each of the Aces, alternately left and right, in overlapping rows. Only the outermost cards in each of these rows is available. These can be placed on the foundation pile if they form the next card in suit and sequence. Alternatively, they can be placed at the outer end of another row, but only in sequence of descending pip value; the suit does not matter. e.g. you can place a 5 of Hearts on a 6 of Spades. If a row is empty, any available card may be placed in it. In this way cards can be moved around, but this is still a tricky game to complete successfully.

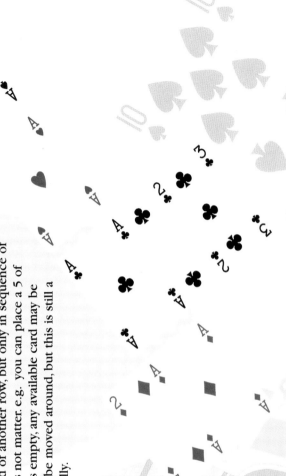

CANFIELD (ALSO KNOWN AS DEMON) **

This game is named after the American in whose casino it was invented.

The Aim: To complete the Foundations and Tableau.

The Method: Use the standard 52-card pack. Deal thirteen cards face-down in one pile, turn the pile face-up and place it at your left to form the stock. Deal the fourteenth card face-up and place it above and to the right of the stock pile. This is the first foundation card. Deal four more cards face-up in a row to the right of the stock, with the first card directly under the first foundation card. These form the tableau. The other three foundation cards are the other cards of the same pip-value as the first one. Place them next to the first, face-up, as they are turned up. The 34 cards remaining after the stock, first foundation card, and tableau cards have been dealt are placed face down, below the tableau. These form the Hand. The top three cards are turned over and laid alongside the hand. Only the top card of these three is available. If playable, it can be played on to a foundation pile or on to the tableau, and the card beneath becomes available. If not playable it forms the first card of the waste pile or talon. Once all possible cards are played, three more are turned over and placed on top of the talon.

When the Hand is exhausted, the talon is turned over, without being shuffled, and becomes the new Hand, cards taken in sets of three as before. This can be repeated indefinitely (sometimes it is restricted to three times only). Foundation piles are built up in suit sequence from the foundation card (e.g. 9, 10, J, Q, K, A, 2, 3, 4, 5, 6, 7, 8). Tableau piles are built up in the sequence of next-lowest rank and opposite colour (e.g. black 7 on top of red 8). A tableau pile must only be moved as a unit, on to a card of next highest rank and opposite colour to the bottom card of the unit. Spaces occurring in the tableau must be filled from the top card of the stock, or from the top of the talon if the stock is exhausted.

CASTLES IN SPAIN ∗∗∗

The Aim: To build up suits, in sequence, from the foundation cards.

The Method: Use the standard 52-card pack. Deal a row of five cards, laying them face down from left to right. Above this row lay a row of four cards, then a row of three above that. Finally place one card above the centre card of the row of three. Then lay down two further sets, also face down, on top of the first set. You have thirteen cards left. Lay them face up, one by one, on top of the existing piles, keeping to the pattern. This makes thirteen depot piles. Any aces showing are played to the foundation row, once the tableau is set out. The card beneath the ace is turned up and becomes available for play. Available cards may be played either on to their foundation pile, or in descending sequence of alternate colour on another depot pile. Sequences or part sequences may be moved from one depot pile to another or to fill any spaces that are created. The cards may not be re-dealt.

CLOCK PATIENCE *

The Aim: To arrange all the cards in clock-face formation, with the Kings in the centre.

The Method: Use the standard 52-card pack. Deal out thirteen packets of four cards, face-down. Place twelve of the packets in a circular formation, corresponding to the numbers on a clock face. Place the thirteenth packet in the centre of the "clock" to form the stock pile. Turn the top card of the stock pile face up.

If it is a Queen, it counts as 12; if a Jack, as 11; the other cards have numbers corresponding to their pip values. The aim is to have them all at the right place on the "clock"; e.g. all four 6's at six o'clock; all four Queens at twelve o'clock. Aces go at one o'clock. Place the turned-up card in the correct position on the clock face, under the packet, face-up, and turn over the top card of that packet. Place that card in its right place in the same way, and turn over the top card of that packet, and so on. If you turn over a King, place him face-up at the bottom of the stock pile, and turn over the top card on the stock pile. Continue until four Kings have been turned up and placed in the stock pile. You win if the last card to be turned up is the fourth King, because by then you will have completed the clock.

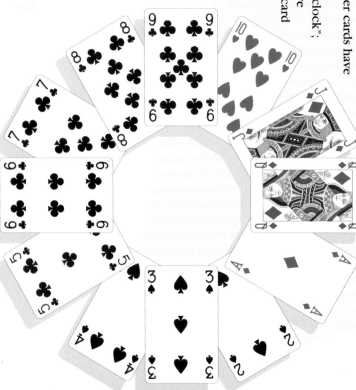

FLOWER GARDEN **

The Aim: To build up each suit in ascending sequence from its Ace (low Ace).

The Method: Use the standard 52-card pack and deal 36 cards, face-up, in 6 columns of 6, overlapping. These are your Garden. The bottom card of each column is available for play. Deal the remaining 16 cards in a face-up row. This is your Bouquet, and all cards in it are available at any time. As Aces become available, place them in a row above the Layout, face-up, and build up on them from 2 to King in each suit. You can create 4 auxiliary columns in which cards may be placed in descending order of suit, with available cards being played to the bottom of the column. When a column is used up, any available card can be used to start a new one.

Note: Only one card is moved at a time. When transferring cards from auxiliary column to foundation pile, cards may only be moved from the top of the auxiliary columns.

GOLF **

The Aim: To completely clear the Tableau.

The Method: Use the standard 52-card pack. Deal a row of seven cards, face-up, then deal four more rows face-up on the first row; making a total of 35 cards, arranged so that all card values can be easily seen.

Turn up the first card from the Hand and lay it down face-up to form the Talon. Any card from the top layer of the tableau pile can be removed and placed on the talon, so long as it is in numerical sequence with the top card, whether upwards or downwards. Cards are turned up from the Hand, or stock, and placed on the talon. Cards in sequence may be played off the tableau on to the talon, so long as each pair of cards is in sequence, upwards or downwards. Suits do not matter. Laying down a King stops the sequence. Aces are low. Only a 2 may be placed on top of an Ace. The game is won if the Tableau can be completely cleared on to the Talon.

Scoring: Treat each deal as a golf hole. Each card remaining in your tableau at the end of a deal counts as a stroke. Par is a total of 36 in nine deals. If the tableau is cleared, any cards remaining in the stock count as one minus-stroke each, and are deducted from the running total.

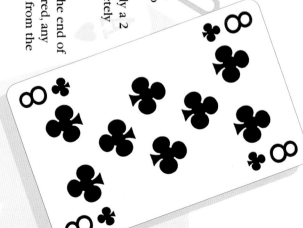

KLONDIKE (ALSO KNOWN AS CANFIELD) **

The Aim: To build up on each Foundation card in suit and sequence, Ace (low) to King.

The Method: Use the standard 52-card pack. Deal one card face up and six others face down in a single row, left to right. Deal a card face-up on top of the second card, then five face-down on top of the others. Deal a card face-up on the third pile, and another four face down, and continue in this way until you have seven piles, the left-hand one consisting of just one card, face-up; the right-hand one consisting of one card face-up and six face-down.

Remaining cards are placed in a packet, face-down, to form the Stock. Aces (the Foundation Cards) should be placed in a row of four, separate from the seven piles, as they appear. Within the Layout, you build sequences of alternating colours - e.g. red, black, red - in descending order - e.g. a red 5 on a black 6, black 7 on red 8. King at the base of the pile. Cards can be transferred to their foundation piles, but cannot then be moved again. All face-up cards on a pile in the Layout must be moved as a unit. Whenever a card, or set of cards, is moved from one file to another, the face-down card that was beneath is turned over, and becomes available for play. When a space is made in the Layout, it can only be filled by a King.

The top card of the Stock (kept face-down) is always available. Normally you would not try using it until you have made all possible moves with the cards in your Layout. You can move a stock card straight into a Foundation pile. If the card from Stock is not usable, it goes into the Waste Pile or Talon, face-up. When the Stock is used up, the talon can be turned over and used as stock. This is done once only.

14

SHAMROCKS **

The Aim: To build complete suit sequences from Ace to King on the Foundation Piles.

The Method: Use the standard 52-card pack. Deal all the cards into seventeen sets of three, spread out in fan-shapes so that suit and pip-value are clearly seen. There will be one single card left. This too goes face-up on the layout. If you have a king and another card of the same suit in one of your fans, put the King below the other. Uncovered cards are available for play. The first move must be to add a card to the single card. No fan is allowed to hold more than three cards. Aces as they appear should be moved beyond the layout, in a row of four, to form the bases of Foundation piles. When you have moved out all the cards from a fan, the space remains empty.

TOWER OF PISA ***

The Aim: To end with a single file of cards descending in sequence from 10 to 2.

The Method: Use the standard 52-card pack, and remove a total of nine number cards, making a complete sequence from 10 to 2, in any mixture of suits. Lay them out in three columns of three. Discard the rest of the pack - it is not required. Once this is done, you can move cards. Only the bottom card of a column can be moved, and it can only be moved to the bottom of another column, and under a card of higher value. An empty file can be filled by the bottom card of either of the other two files.

Note: If you start with a 10 on the bottom row, try to use all the cards from one of the files, in order to have an empty file. Now you can move the 10 to the top (so long as it is still at the bottom of its file after your previous moves).

GAMES FOR TWO OR MORE PLAYERS

AUCTION PITCH **

This game is also known as Setback.

Number of Players: Two to eight, but four is best.

The Aim: To be first to gain seven points.

The Method: Use the standard 52-card pack. Aces are high. Cut for dealer (highest card). Dealer deals six cards to each player, from the left, in batches of three at at a time. Each player, beginning with eldest hand, bids for the number of points he expects to make in play. Each new bid must be higher than the previous one, except that the dealer, as last bidder need only match the previous bid, so long as it is less than four points. Players may pass rather than bid, and if all pass, the cards are gathered, shuffled and re-dealt by the same dealer. The highest bidder then declares trumps by "pitching" a card of that suit on to the table, face-up. Other players must follow suit if they can, or play a trump. Highest trump takes the trick, and the winner leads to the next trick. If a trump is again led, the same rule applies. If another suit is led, players may either follow suit or trump, but they can discard only if unable to follow suit. The highest card of the led suit wins, unless it is trumped. Play goes round until all tricks are taken.

Scoring: One point is given for each of:

High: The highest trump card played.

Low: The lowest trump card played.

Jack: The Jack of trumps.

Game: The highest value of scoring cards. The scoring cards are Ace (4); King (3); Queen (2);Jack (1) and 10 (10). Other cards have no scoring value. If the Jack is also highest or lowest trump played, it gets the extra points. If a bidder fails to gain his bid, he is set back by the difference between his actual and his forecast score, which may end up in a minus figure, in which case he is "in the hole". The game is won by the first player to reach seven points, though by agreement this figure can be increased to a higher total. If two player make or exceed seven and one is the pitcher, the pitcher wins. If neither is the pitcher, the scores of each are counted in order to see who made seven first. No game point is given if two players tie for it.

Bidding "Smudge": A player who bids four, and makes it, is said to gain a smudge, or slam, and is awarded enough points to win the game outright (and any stakes that have been wagered). The only exception to this is if he was in the hole when making the bid, in which case he gains only the four points.

AUTHORS *

Number of Players: From three to six, but four or five make the best number.
The Aim: To collect the most "books", i.e. sets of four cards all of the same rank.

The Method: Use the standard 52-card pack. Cut for dealer (highest card). The dealer deals out the full pack among the players; some may end up with a card less, but this does not matter. Play starts with the player to the left of the dealer. Looking at his hand, he decides what card to ask for. It must be of a rank in which he already has at least one card, from a different suit. He then chooses an opponent and addresses him by name, e. g. "George, please give me the 7 of Clubs". If George has that card, he must hand it over, and the asker's turn goes on until he asks for a card which an opponent does not have. The turn then passes to his left. When a player has all four cards of the same rank, he lays them face-down on the table, as a book. The winner is the one with most books. If playing for stakes, the winner of each book collects a chip from the other players. If a player asks for a card he already holds, or does not pass over a requested card when he has it, he pays a chip to each of the other players.

18

BEGGAR YOUR NEIGHBOUR *

Number of Players: Two.

The Aim: To win all 52 cards.

The Method: Use the standard pack of 52 cards. Cut for dealer (higher card). The non-dealer shuffles the cards. Each receives 26 cards. The cards should be set out in a pile, face down. Each player turns over the top card and places it in front of his pile. The higher card wins the other (Aces are low), and the player takes both cards and puts them face down. If two cards of the same value are turned over, then a 'war' is declared. The two equal cards are placed in the centre of the table. Each player makes a pile of three cards placed face-down, with a fourth on top, face-up. The higher of the face-up cards wins both piles, plus the two cards in the centre. If the two face-up cards are of equal value, the war is repeated, and the winner takes all the cards played. The game goes on until one player has all the cards.

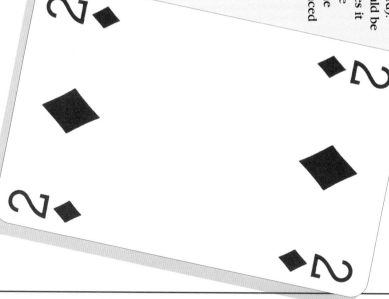

BLACKJACK ***

This game is the US form of Pontoon (see page 48).

Number of Players: Three to twelve, but four to six is best.

The Aim: To hit a total of 21, or as close as possible beneath it.

Card values: Ace: 1 or 11; King, Queen, Jack all 10; other cards by pip value.

The Method: Use the standard 52-card pack. Aces can be high or low. Cut or draw for dealer (lowest card). Dealer then deals a single card to each player, including himself. Having seen his card, each player places a bet on it (antes), up to an agreed maximum. The banker does not bet, but may double: if he does, any player unwilling to go double loses his stake. Players may also redouble. The banker then deals a second card all round. Any player then holding an Ace (11) or a court card or a 10 (10) has a "Natural 21" and the banker pays him double his stake, unless the banker also has a natural. In that case, the banker collects the player's stake, plus double the stake of any player who does not hold a natural. If no player has a natural, the banker then deals further cards from left, face-up, as the player calls for them.

The aim is to get to 21, or as near as possible, without going over (bust). The player can call "Stand" when he wants to stop, or say "Twist", or "Hit Me" if he wants to continue receiving cards. If the player is bust, the banker gets his stake. Players who have chosen to stand wait until the banker has dealt further cards to himself. If the banker goes bust, he pays the stake back to each standing player. If the dealer too stands, then each player shows his full Hand. The dealer pays off players with a total higher than his own (but less than 22) and collects from any with a lesser or the same total as himself.

Splitting: Players can split pairs, if his first two cards are of the same number value and rank (i.e. two Kings may be split, but not a King and a 10); he turns up the first card and treats each card as a separate Hand, on which he can draw, or stand. He must bet equally on each split Hand.

Doubling Down: If a player's first two cards come to a total of 11, he can turn up his first card up, and call for another card to replace it, also doubling his bet. He must then stand on these three cards. The deal normally stays with the original banker, but he can sell the bank to the highest bidder before or after any Hand. But if a player has a natural, and the banker does not, then the player with the natural takes over the bank in the next hand. If more than one player has a natural, the one nearest the banker's left takes precedence.

BLACK MARIA ✱✱

Number of Players: From three to six.

The Aim: To win tricks without winning any cards from the Hearts suit, or the Queen of Spades (Black Maria).

The Method: Use the standard pack of 52, but with three players, take out the 2 of Clubs. Always make sure that equal numbers of cards are dealt. Aces are high. Cut for dealer (lowest card). Dealing goes to the left. All cards are dealt out, one at a time. Once a player has seen his hand, he can place any three cards face-down, to be picked up by the player on his left; and he must pick up three from the player on his right. The opening lead is made by the player on the dealer's left. Other players must follow suit if they can; otherwise any card may be played. There are no trumps. The highest card of the leading suit wins. The winning player leads to the next player on the left. After each hand, the deal moves to the next player on the left.

Scoring: The aim is to avoid collecting hearts and to lose any Hearts that one is dealt. Each time a player takes a heart, he loses a point. At the end of the round, each player adds his score of Hearts, adding one for each Heart card he has. The lowest score wins the round. The game continues until one player reaches a score of fifty. The player with the lowest score is the winner.

Penalty Card: The Queen of Spades is treated as an additional Heart, but counting for 20 points.

Bonus card: The Jack of Diamonds can be treated as a bonus card, allowing a deduction of 10 points.

BRAG **

The most common form of Brag is Three-Card Brag.

Number of Players: Three to six.

The Aim: To win the pool by ending with the strongest Hand.

The Method: Use the standard 52-card pack. Aces are high, except for Ace, 2 3; when they are low. Stake limits are agreed at the start and cards are cut to find the dealer (highest card, with Ace high). Dealer antes his agreed stake, and deals three cards, one at a time, face-down, to each player. The remainder go face-up to his left.

Eldest Hand is first to bet, and may do so without looking at his cards. If he looks, he can then bet (holding his Hand) or drop out, in which case he places his cards on top of the stock. If he bets blind, he does not touch his cards. The turn passes to the left, and the player has the same choices, though if he bets it must be an amount equal to or greater than the previous bet, unless he is betting "open" and the previous bet was blind. In that case, he must bet at least double the previous one. If he bets blind and the one before him was open, he need only bet half. In a later round, a player may switch from betting blind to betting open. If he then decides to drop out, his cards go on the stock and his stake is lost. A player betting the same amount as the

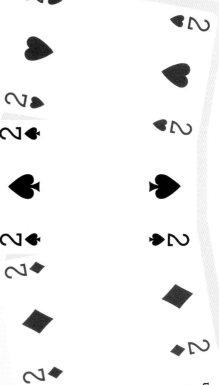

previous bet says "Stay" and names the sum. A player increasing the bet says "Raise" and names the sum. Play continues until only two players remain in play. If both are playing open, either may call to see the other's Hand, so long as he is at least matching the other's previous stake. On seeing the other Hand, the caller may then drop out, without showing his own Hand, and lose; or show that he has a better hand, and win. If one player is betting blind and the other is betting open, then the player betting open must continue to double the blind player's stake, or drop out. If both are betting blind, play continues until one does look at his cards. However it is possible for one blind player to call another; but not for an open player to call a blind one. The winner takes the pool.

Scoring:

Prial: Three of the same rank, e.g. 2-2-2.

Flush Run: Three in suit and sequence, e.g. 2-3-4 of Hearts.

Run: Any three in sequence, e.g. 2-3-4 of mixed suits.

Flush: Any three in the same suit.

Pair: Two of same rank plus a singleton, e.g. 2-2-9

High Card: No combination, but highest card, or second or third if there is a tie, wins.

In Pairs, a higher pair beats a lower pair, and equal pairs are decided by the singleton. Some players take a prial of 3-3-3 as beating Queen-King-Ace.

AMERICAN BRAG

In this form all Jacks and all 9's are Bragger's. These are all equal in value, and the highest Hand is a Hand of three bragger's. A combination including a bragger outranks a natural Hand of the same value. American Brag is more likely to result in a tie, in which case the pool is divided evenly.

BRIDGE ***

Also called Contract Bridge

Number of Players: Four, playing as two partnerships.

The Aim: To be the first side to win two games.

Method: Use the standard 52-card pack. Aces are high. It is usual to have a second pack, ready-shuffled, for the next dealer. Players sit with partners facing each other: North-South; East-West. Cut or draw for dealer. Before each deal, the pack is cut by the player to the dealer's right. The dealer then deals 13 cards to each player.

Bidding: Also known as the Auction, this starts with the dealer, who bids for the number of tricks he expects to take, along with his partner. He also specifies the trump suit, or states, "No trump". E.g. "Four Spades" means he expects to score four tricks with Spades as trumps. Scoring only begins after six tricks have been won, and the lowest bid is One (i.e. one more than six). Bids run in ascending order: Clubs, Diamonds (the minor suits) Hearts, Spades (major suits), and No Trumps. Lowest bid is one Club; highest is seven No Trumps. Alternatively, a bidder can Pass (no tricks over six). Bidding moves to the left. If all pass, Hands are turned in and the deal moves to the left. If a bid is made, the next player can raise it (e.g. from one Spade to two Spades) or go higher (e.g. one Heart over one Diamond). A player may double a bid made by the opposing team: this means that if they make the bid, they score double trick points; if they fail, the opposing side gets the trick points. The next player to call can over call (make a higher bid) or redouble the already-doubled bid, which redoubles the potential gain for either side. Players do not double or redouble their own partner's bids. Players may re-bid, but when three have "passed" in a row, bidding stops.

At the end of bidding, the last to bid becomes the Declarer, and plays the Hand for the bidding team, unless he names the same trump suit (or no trumps) as his partner did, in which case the partner becomes Declarer. The declaring side must win at least as many tricks as they bid; the defending side tries to prevent them. Play begins with the opponent on the declarer's left, who leads with any card. The declarer's partner then lays his hand face-up on the table, arranging it in suits, in descending order from the Aces. This enables the declarer to play it as a "dummy" Hand whilst also playing his own Hand: his partner cannot assist. Play goes to the left; players must follow suit if they can; otherwise they may either trump or play a discard. Highest card of the suit led, or highest trump, takes the trick. The winner of the trick leads to the next, and so on until all thirteen tricks are taken.

Scoring: tricks are scored in ascending value, according to the trump suit, or No Trumps. In Clubs and Diamonds, each trick scored (from the 7th) counts as 20 points. In Hearts and Spades, each trick scored counts as 30 points. With No Trumps, the first trick scored is at 40 points, with 30 points for each additional bid. If the bid has been doubled, the scores are doubled, and multiplied by 4 if redoubled. The first side to score 100 trick points wins, and play resumes in a fresh game. The rubber ends if the same team wins two games in a row; otherwise it is best of three.

Scoring Method: Both sides keep the score for the other side as well as for themselves, to ensure accuracy. A special sheet is used, or can be drawn up, with a column for each side (WE and THEY) and a horizontal line across the middle. Trick points (including doubles) are entered below this line, and bonus points above it. Bonus points are awarded for tricks won over and above the contract; for winning a contract to take 12 tricks (Small Slam) or 13 tricks (Grand Slam); and for defeating a contract. Bonus points are also awarded to players who happen to get the honour cards (Ace down to 10) of the trump suit, or all four Aces if the call is No Trumps. This applies to the player's own hand, not to the combined hands of the partnership.

The side to win the first game of a rubber is then called "vulnerable" and different scoring rates apply to it (see Scoring Table).

Scoring Table for Contract Bridge

Declarer's side, below the line score

For each odd trick over six	Ordinary Contract	Doubled	Redoubled
Minor Suits	20	40	80
Major Suits	30	60	120
No Trump: first trick	40	80	120
Further tricks	30	60	120

Declarer's side, above the line score

	Not vulnerable Minor Major & NT		Vulnerable Minor Major & NT		Making Contract
Each overtrick	20	30	20	30	No bonus
When doubled	100	100	200	200	50
When redoubled	200	200	400	400	50
Small Slam	500	500	750	750	
Grand Slam	1000	1000	1500	1500	

Defender's above the line score when Declarers fail to make contract

	Not vulnerable All Suits & NT	Vulnerable All Suits & NT
Each undertrick	50	100
Doubled: 1st undertrick	100	200
Each further undertrick	200	400
Redoubled: 1st	200	400
Each further undertrick	400	600

Winner's Bonus Points (Above the Line)

	Win Rubber in 2 Games	Rubber in 2 out of 3 Games	One Game, Rubber Unfinished	Part Score, Rubber Unfinished
	700	500	300	50

Bonus Points for Honour Cards Held

Trump Suit		No Trumps (All the Aces) All in one hand
4 in one hand	5 in one hand	
100	150	150

Conventions: Effective bridge play means that the players in the two partnerships must use the same "language"; during the auction they cannot see each other's Hands and have to rely on applying the same bidding pattern to get an understanding of what each is holding. There are numerous systems, and entire books have been written about each one. Probably the most straightforward is to assign points to individual cards, once you have sorted your hand into its suits, in descending order of value from left to right. Count 4 for each Ace, three for each King, two for each Queen and one for each Jack. These are your high-card points. Normally a partnership will have a combined strength of around 20. With 25 in high cards you should win the game; with 37 you should achieve a Grand Slam. If your high cards come to less than 13, leave the opening bid to your partner.

Four or more cards of the same suit in your Hand make a long suit; 3 or less a short suit. Count an extra point for any fourth or more card in a side (non-trump) suit, and any fifth or more card in a trump suit. To open with a suit bid of one (naming trumps) you should hold 12 to 14 points in that suit. With two biddable suits, bid the longer; if they are of equal length, bid the higher-scoring one. For a trump bid of two, you need at least 7 cards in your trump suit and a value of 22. This is a very strong signal to your partner.

The most common opening bid is one trick, and the partner's responding bid must convey a message back about the strength of his own Hand, which will then determine what happens in the next round of bidding. He can raise in the same suit, make a higher bid in a new suit, or bid No Trumps. If he has at least three cards of the first bidder's named trump suit, he can safely raise the bid to two. Cautious bidding should be the rule until you have got a feeling for the game - and an understanding with your partner. It is a good idea to practice bidding patterns outside the framework of an actual game.

Catch the Ten, or Scotch Whist *

Number of Players: Two to eight.

The Aim: To win tricks, especially with the top five trumps.

The Method: Use a 36-card pack, with Ace high, and 2 to 5 omitted. Remove any 6 if five to seven are playing; include the 5 if eight are playing. Cut for dealer (highest card). Dealer deals out the full pack, one card at a time, giving a total of nine each if four are playing; seven each to five; six each to six; and five each to seven or eight. The dealer turns up the final card to show trumps, before taking in into his own Hand.

Eldest Hand leads, and other players, from the left, must follow suit if they can, otherwise trump or play a discard. The trick is won by the highest card of the suit led, or by the highest trump. The winner of a trick leads to the next.

Scoring: The top five cards in the trump suit are: Jack (11); Ace (4); King (3); Queen (2) and 10 (10). No other cards have value. When all tricks are taken, each player counts the value of the trumps in his set of tricks, and also adds one point for every card he now has in addition to the cards he was originally dealt.

CHEAT!   *

Number of Players: Three upwards.

The Aim: To be first to get rid of all the cards in your Hand.

The Method: Use the standard 52-card pack. Cut for dealer (highest card). The dealer deals all the cards among the players, one at a time. The player to the dealer's left leads, by placing face-down one or more cards. He says what the cards are - but he is not obliged to tell the truth about the number of cards, their suit or their value. An opposing player may call "Cheat!" at any point. The last player has then to turn his discards face-up. If it turns out that he was cheating, he has to pick up all the cards in the discard pile. If he was not, the caller must take all the discards. If there is no call, the next player to the left takes his turn, placing his cards face-down on top of the cards already played. He can play only cards of the same value as those just announced, or the next rank up (Ace if it was a King, 2 if it was an Ace). But - he may cheat. The game goes on in this way until one player has successfully laid down all his cards.

cheat !

CRAZY EIGHTS **

Number of Players: Can be played by two, but three to five is better, and seven or more is possible.

The Aim: To be first to get rid of all one's cards, and to reach 500 points.

The Method: Use the standard 52-pack; two packs shuffled together if seven or more are playing. Cut for dealer (highest card). Dealer deals five cards to each player, from his left, one at a time. The remaining cards form the stock, face-down, with the top card turned face-up and laid alongside to start the discard pile. Starting with the player on the dealer's left, each player either puts down a playable card face-up on the discard pile, or, if no card is available, draws an additional card from stock. Playable cards depend on what the top card on the discard pile is. If it is not an 8, any card may be played which matches the suit or is equal in rank. If it is an 8, then any card of the same suit may be played. An 8 may be played at any time, and the player who leads it can name any suit to go next. The first player to go out (i.e. put down all his cards) calls out "Crazy eights!" and wins the round. First player to reach 500 points wins the game.

Scoring: The winner of a round scores 100.
Penalty scores for players with cards in hand are as follows:
Eight: 50
Any Court card: 10
Other cards: Face value

Variants: To add a touch of complexity, a player who is down to one card must knock on the table to indicate this, or else pick up two cards from the stock. If the player before you puts down a Queen (or other previously decided card) you miss that turn. When an Ace is played, reverse the direction of play.

FAN-TAN ✳✳

Number of Players: Three to Eight.

The Aim: To get rid of all your cards.

The Method: Each player starts off with an equal number of chips, and puts a chip into the pool at the start. Use the standard pack of 52 cards. Choose the dealer by someone dealing cards face-up; the first dealer by someone dealing cards face-up; the first to get a Jack becomes the dealer. The dealer shuffles, and player to his right cuts. Cards are dealt one at a time, from the dealer's left, until the pack is used up. Play begins from the dealer's left. The first card to be played must be a 7. If you have no seven you pass, and pay a chip to the pool. When a 7 is put down, the 6 and 8 of the same suit are also available for play, and once these are down, the next values above and below can be played. The four 7's are laid in a row in the centre of the table, with the 6's to one side and the 8's to the other. Suits can then be built up to the King and down to the Ace, which is low. Only one card can be played in each turn. If you can play a card, you must. If you pass when able to play, pay a penalty of three chips to the pool. The first player to lay down all his cards wins. Others pay one chip for each card they are left holding; and the winner then takes the whole pool.

FIVE HUNDRED   ★ ★ ★

Number of Players: Two to six, but three is the ideal number.

The Aim: To make, or beat, the contract; and be first to score 500 points.

The Method: Use a pack of 32 cards (standard pack excluding all cards between 2 and 6, inclusive), plus a Joker. Draw for first deal: lowest card wins (Ace is low, Joker lowest). Deal to the left, ten cards to each player in packets of 3-4-3. After the first round of 3, three cards are laid face-down in the centre. This is the widow. Having seen their Hands, each player may make a single bid, or pass. Each bid states the number of tricks the player will take, from six to ten; and his trump suit (or No Trumps), e. g. "eight diamonds"; "ten no trump". Each bid must be for a higher number of tricks than the bid before, or the same number if ten. The highest bid, or first to bid ten, becomes the contract. If no-one makes a bid, the dealt cards are collected, shuffled and re-dealt by the next dealer (player to the dealer's left). Bidding then resumes. The other two players combine in alliance to defeat the bidder, but they may not see each other's Hands. The bidder takes up the widow, then discards any three cards from his Hand. He can lead with any card. The others must follow suit, if able; if they can't, any card may be played. The trick is won by the highest trump, or highest card of the suit led. The winner of the trick leads to the next trick. If the bidder had called No Trumps, then the only trump is the Joker. The trick can only be won by the highest card of the suit led, unless the Joker is played, when it wins. If a player leads with the Joker, he must declare the suit that the others must follow, if they can.

Trumps: The ranking of suits, high to low, is: Hearts, Diamonds, Clubs, Spades. But a No Trump bid outranks them all.

Card ranking in the trump suit: Joker; Jack; Jack of the other suit of the same colour; ace; King; Queen; 10; 9; 8; 7.

Card ranking in the non-trump suits: Ace, King, Queen, Jack (but see above); 10; 9; 8; 7.

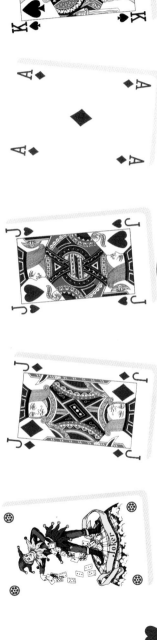

Scoring: Each player keeps a running total from round to round. The bidder's opponents keep their scores separately.

See the table for the number of points awarded.

If the bidder makes his contract, he scores the value of his bid. If his bid adds up to less than 250, and he actually takes all ten tricks, he is awarded only 250. If he is set back (fails to make his contract), then the value of his bid is subtracted from his running total. This can produce a minus figure. Each opponent scores 10 points for every trick he wins.

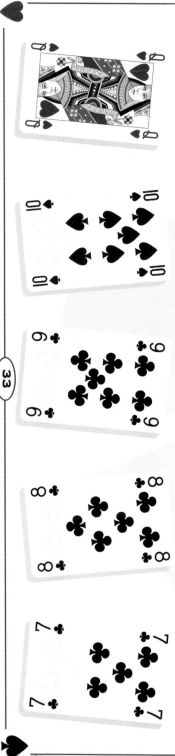

	NUMBER OF TRICKS BID				
	6	7	8	9	10
NO TRUMP	120	220	320	420	520
HEARTS	100	200	300	400	500
DIAMONDS	80	180	280	380	480
CLUBS	60	160	260	360	460
SPADES	40	140	240	340	440

Game is made at 500. If another player goes out (hits 500) in the same deal as the bidder, the bidder wins.

Variant. A player may bid "nullo". This is an offer to win no tricks, at No Trump. Its scoring value is 250, so its bid value is between eight clubs and eight spades. If the nullo bidder gains the contract, he loses if he wins a single trick. Each opponent gains 10 points for each trick made by the bidder.

FROGS IN THE POND *

Number of Players: Two.

The Aim: To be first to score 100 points, by winning tricks.

The Method: Use the standard 52-card pack. Cut for dealer (highest card). The dealer deals ten cards to each, two at a time. He then deals ten cards face down in the centre of the table: these are the "frogs in the pond".

The dealer then leads a single card. The opponent must follow suit, from his ten cards; if he cannot the penalty is 10 points, and the dealer takes the trick. Alternatively, if the opponent can follow suit, he wins 10 points.

The winner of each trick takes the cards played, plus one frog, which goes face down on the trick gained. The winner then leads for the next trick.

There are no trumps.

Players keep the tricks they have won. When all cards are played, the score - including frogs - is added up, and another round begins.

Scoring: The only cards with scoring value are Tens: 10; Fives: 5; Aces: 4; Kings: 3; Queens: 2; Jacks: 1. All others: nil.

Note: In the basic version you only have to follow suit to win the trick, even if you play a lower card. It is also possible to play so that the higher card in the led suit wins the trick.

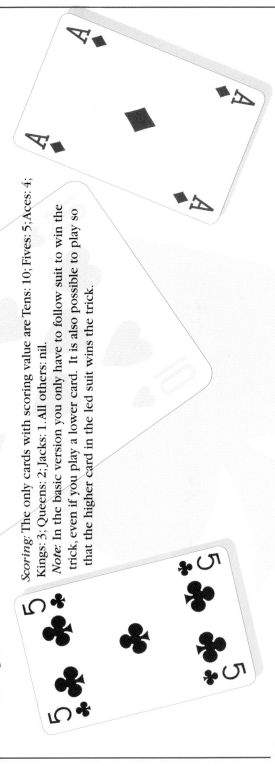

GERMAN WHIST **

Number of Players: Two

The Aim: To build a winning Hand and score 50 points.

The Method: Use the standard 52-card pack. Cut for dealer (highest card). Dealer then deals 13 cards alternately to each player. The 27th card is turned over to denote trumps for the game. The remaining cards form the stock, face down. The dealer leads a card, and the opponent can either beat it with a higher card of the same suit, or any trump (if trumps were not played), or play a lower card and lose the trick. The winner of the first trick takes the face-up trump card, waits for his opponent to draw a fresh card from the stock, then turns over the next card. When all the stock has been played, the players' hands are played out, with the winner of the previous trick taking the lead.

Scoring: One point per trick. The winning score is normally 50, though this can be varied by agreement.

GIN RUMMY **

Number of Players: Two.

The Aim: To build up a winning Hand of Melds and be first to score 100 points.

The Method: Use the standard 52-card pack (Ace is low). Cut for dealer.

Dealer shuffles, and deals ten cards to each player. The remaining cards are placed face-down to form the stock. The top card is turned face-up, and placed by itself, to start the discard pile. The other player has the option of taking that card, or refusing it; he cannot draw a card from the stock pile. If he refuses it, the turn goes to the dealer. If the dealer also passes (refuses the turned-up card) the other player may take the top (face-down) card from stock. When a card is picked up, another must be placed on the discard pile.

The aim is to be the first to lay down all your cards in melds (sets of three or more cards of the same suit in consecutive numbers, counting from Ace as low; or sets of three or more from different suits but the same value). If you have a full hand of melds, call out "Gin!" or knock on the table. You receive a bonus of 25 points plus the value of your opponent's unmelded cards. You can also choose to go out if you have some melds and the unmelded cards in your hand have a value of 10 points or less. In this case, however, your opponent has the chance to "lay off" available cards on your melds, and complete his melds using your unmelded cards before the score is counted. The player with the lower value of unmelded cards receives a 25 point bonus. If neither player has gone out before the last two cards are drawn from the stock, the round is treated as a no-score draw.

Scoring: Court Cards (King, Queen, Jack): 10 points each. Ace: one point. Number cards: as their number value. The value of the unmatched or unmelded cards still in your hand counts against you. If the player who went out has the same, or greater value of remaining cards as his opponent, the opponent gets a ten-point bonus plus the difference between the card values. The winner of the game is the first to reach 100 points.

GIN!

GO BOOM ✽

Number of Players: Two to six.

The Aim: To be first to get rid of all one's cards.

The Method: Use the standard pack of 52 cards. Cut for dealer (highest card). The dealer deals seven cards, one at a time, to each player. The rest of the pack is placed face-down and forms the stock. Eldest Hand (the player to the dealer's left) leads. Other players must follow suit, or play a card of the same face value as the lead (Aces are high). A player who has no playable card must draw from the stock until he receives a playable card. Once the stock is used up, players with no playable card must pass (wait for the next trick to be played). The trick is won by the highest card of the suit led. The winner of a trick leads to the next trick. Tricks are piled into a discard pile since they have no scoring value. The first player to have no cards left is the one who "Goes Boom" and wins the game.

HONEST JOHN *

Number of Players: From two to twelve.

The Aim: To bet on the chance of turning up a higher card than the banker's.

The Method: Use the standard pack of 52 cards. Aces are high. Cut for dealer, who is also banker (highest card). Dealer cuts the pack into from four to six separate piles, face-down. Each player places a chip against his chosen pile, leaving one pile vacant for the banker. The banker turns over the top card of his pile. From the banker's left, the players now turn over the top cards of their piles, in turn. For any card that is of lower value than the banker's, or matches it, they pay their chip to the banker. The banker pays a chip for any card of higher value than his own. All suits are equal. The bank moves to the left after each hand is completed.

KNAVES *

Number of Players: Three.

The Aim: To win the greatest number of tricks, without taking any Jacks.

The Method: Use the standard 52-card pack. Aces are high. Cut for dealer (highest card). The dealer deals seventeen cards to each player, one card at a time. The left-over card is turned over to denote trumps for the round. The player to the dealer's left leads by laying down a card. Other players must follow suit, trump, or discard a card.

Scoring: Each trick won receives one point. The first player to reach twenty points wins the game. But any trick containing a Jack is penalised by deducting points as follows: Jack of Hearts four; Diamonds three; Clubs two; Spades one.

KNOCK-OUT WHIST ✳

Number of Players: From three upwards.

Aim of the Game: To win the greatest number of tricks.

How to Play: Use the 52-card pack. Aces are high. Cut for dealer (highest card). The dealer then deals seven cards to each player. The rest of the cards are placed face-down, but the top one is turned over to determine trumps. Aces are high. The player to the dealer's left leads the first card. Players must follow suit if they can, otherwise they may play any card. In the second round six cards are dealt (and five in the third round, down to one in the final round). The winner of a round calls trumps for the next, after the deal. In the seventh round, when only one card is dealt to each player, the players cut for trumps.

A player who takes no tricks in any round is "knocked" out and takes no more part in the game. However, the first player to take no tricks is awarded the "dog's chance". He is dealt one card in the next round, and can play it to the trick of his choice. If he does not play it to a particular trick, he knocks on the table, and play passes to the next in turn. If he wins a trick, he is fully back in the game for the next round. The game can be won in any round after the third if one player takes all the tricks.

Loo *

Number of Players: From three to nine.

The Aim: To win tricks.

The Method 1: Single Pool. Use the standard pack of 52 cards. Aces are high.

Players put an agreed number of chips or coins into the pool. These must always be equally divisible by three.

Any player distributes cards until a Jack is dealt: the recipient of the Jack is first dealer.

Trumps are not determined immediately. If all players are able to follow suit in each of the three leads, trumps are not called. But as soon as someone fails to follow suit, once that trick is completed, then the top card of the stock pile is turned face-up to determine trumps for each subsequent trick. Three cards are dealt, one at a time, to each player, starting to the dealer's left. The player to the dealer's left leads. Others must follow suit if they can, otherwise they may trump (see above). Tricks are not gathered together: the cards are left face-up in front of the players.

Scoring: Each winning trick is entitled to win one third of the pool in each round. Players with no tricks are looed. They must put a double stake into the pool for the next round.

Method 2: Double Pool. In this method, an extra hand, known as the Miss, is dealt, to the right of the dealer. The top card of the stock is turned up to determine trumps. Before the opening lead, each player must tell the dealer whether he will stand, pass, or take the Miss. To stand is to remain in play, and participate in the tricks. To pass is to go out of play: the player's cards are placed face-down under the stock. To take the Miss is to pick up the extra hand and to place your original hand face-down under the stock. If you take the Miss you cannot then pass, and must remain in play. If all players pass except the dealer, or a player who has taken the Miss, the lone player takes the whole pool. If only one player ahead of the dealer stands, then the dealer must either stand, or take the Miss, and "defend" the pool. In Double Pool the player leader to each trick must play a trump if he has one; and if he has the Ace of trumps, that must be led first. If the Ace was turned up and he has the King, then that must be led first.

Scoring: As before, with each trick taking one third of the pool. Where the dealer has had to "defend" the pool, he neither collects nor pays, but his opponent, depending on his score, does one or the other.

NAP, OR NAPOLEON **

Number of Players: From two to six, but four or five make the best game.

The Aim: As highest bidder, to win the contracted number of tricks.

The Method: Use the standard pack of 52 cards. Aces are high, except when drawing for the deal, when they are low. Lowest card is first to deal and has choice of seat, with second-lowest on his left, and so on. Players pay an agreed number of tokens or coins into the pool. The dealer deals out five cards, one at a time, to each player, starting on his left. On receipt of the cards, each player, starting on the dealer's left, must make a bid for the number of tricks that he will win, if he gets the chance to name the trump suit. Each must either bid higher than the previous bid, or pass. If all pass, the dealer must make the minimal bid of at least one trick. Otherwise, the lowest acceptable bid is two. To bid for all five tricks is to go Nap. The highest bidder makes the opening lead, and the suit he leads automatically becomes trumps. Others must follow suit if they can, or play a discard. The highest trump, or if No Trump is played in following suits, the highest card of the leading suit wins. The winner leads to the next trick. The other players set out to play against the highest bidder. If the highest bidder wins tricks over and above his bid, he receives no credit. As soon as he has won his forecast number of tricks, he must show his remaining cards to prove that he has not revoked at any point.

Scoring: If Nap is made, it is worth ten points to the winner. If, having bid Nap, the player fails to make it, he pays five points to the other players. If the player makes his bid, but it is less than Nap, it is worth as many points as there are tricks; if he is defeated, he pays the same number of points, to each of his opponents.

Deals are settled at the end of each round.

Note: 1. Bidding can be increased if players are allowed to bid a Wellington. This is a bid to go Nap, but also doubling all the stakes. A player can only do this if Nap has already been bid.

2. Bidding misère. This is a bid to take no tricks, which can be made by a player with no trumps. It exceeds a bid for three tricks but is itself exceeded by a bid for four. It offers a player with a poor hand an opportunity to stay in the game.

OH HELL ✳✳

Number of Players: From three to seven can play, but four are best.

The Aim: To achieve exactly the number of tricks you predict or "bid".

The Method: Use the standard 52-card pack. Each player plays for himself alone; there are no partners. Cut for dealer (highest card); dealer also chooses where to sit. Others sit from the dealer's left in descending order of card drawn. The first deal is one card each. Each subsequent deal is increased by one card each until the thirteenth and last, when the full pack is dealt out (always in equal hands: leftover cards in the last deal are not used). After each deal, except the last one, the next card is turned up to determine trumps. In the final deal there are no trumps. Each player, starting from dealer's left, must make a bid, predicting the number of tricks he will take. This can include Zero, or Pass. Bids, also known as Contracts, are recorded on paper by a score keeper, who at the end of bidding announces whether the total number of bids is Over, Under or Even with the number of winnable tricks in the round. The player to the dealer's left leads. Other players must follow suit, or if unable to do so, may play any card including a trump. The winner of a trick leads to the next trick.

Scoring: A player who achieves his exact Contract scores ten, plus the amount of his bid. A player who achieves either more or less than his bid "busts" and receives no points.

42

OLD MAID ✲

Number of Players: Two to five.

The Aim: To avoid being left holding the last remaining Queen.

The Method: Cut for dealer (highest card). Set aside the Queen of Clubs from a 52-card deck, and deal out the remaining 51 cards (no matter if one player has an extra card). Each player's cards are spread out, face-up, and any pairs are removed and placed face-up in the centre of the table. Players take it in turn, left to right, to lay their cards on the table, face-down, holds them facing away from the others. Players then shuffles his remaining cards and for the player to the left to select one. If it enables him to make a pair, he discards the pair; if not, he keeps it.

Then it is his turn to offer his cards to the player on his left. Eventually all the cards will be paired except for the one remaining Queen - The Old Maid - and whoever is left with it loses the round. Play continues for an agreed number of rounds, with the winner being the one to win the most rounds.

PIP-PIP *

Number of Players: Three to seven.

The Aim: To score points for changing the trump suit, and for capturing certain cards.

The Method: Use two standard 52-card packs, thoroughly shuffled together. Cut for dealer (highest card), and cut again to identify trumps. Dealer deals seven cards to each player and places the remainder face-down as the stock. Eldest hand leads to the first trick and others must follow suit if they can, or trump, or discard from another suit. The trick is taken by the highest card of the suit led, or by the highest trump (see Scoring values). If two identical cards are played, the second beats the first.

The winner of a trick draws the top card from the stock and adds it to his hand, and other players, from his left, do the same. When there are not enough cards left in the stock to go round, no more cards are drawn, and hands are played until all cards are gone.

Changing trumps: Just before a card is led to a new trick, a player with a King and Queen of the same suit (so long as it is not the trump suit) in his hand can turn that suit into trumps by saying "Pip-pip", and laying the cards face-down on the table. They continue to be playable as part of his hand. This earns a bonus of 50 points.

If two players call "Pip-pip" before the same trick, both get 50 points, but the later call becomes trumps. A player can call "Pip-pip" twice for the same suit, so long as he has both Kings and both Queens.

PIP-PIP !

Scoring: The only cards with scoring values are:
2's (deuces): 11; Aces: 10; Kings: 5; Queens: 4; Jacks: 3. Others: nil.
Each player adds up his card-score and his piping score at the end of each round, and the highest score is the winner.

44

POKER * * *

There are two basic forms of Poker; Draw and Stud Poker, and each has many variants. However, there are certain standard features, and once you know these, it are easy to learn any adaptation of the game.

Number of Players: 3 or more. Five to eight is best for Draw Poker, seven to ten for Stud Poker.

The Aim: To have the highest-ranking hand at the end of the game.

The Method: Use the standard 52-card pack. Aces can be high or low. The suits are all of equal value.

Scoring: All poker hands consist of five cards. Depending on your hand, you score it as follows (highest to lowest):

Straight Flush: Five cards in suit and sequence, with Ace being either high or low.

A Royal Flush: (Ace-high, King, Queen,Jack, 10 straight flush) beats any other.

Four of a Kind: Four cards of the same value (e.g. four Queens or four 4's), plus any other card. A higher-ranking set beats a lower-ranking one.

Full House: Three of one kind and a pair of another kind (e.g. three Queens and two 4's). A higher-ranking set beats a lower-ranking one.

Flush: Five cards all of the same suit but not making up a complete sequence. If two players have flushes, the one with the higher top card wins. If the top cards match, then highest second card wins, and so on.

Straight: Five cards in complete sequence of rank, with Ace either high or low, but of different suits. Higher top card beats a lower one.

Three of a Kind: Three cards of the same value, plus two others which are not a pair. A higher-ranking set beats a lower-ranking one.

Two Pairs: Two sets of two of the same value, plus any other card. Highest ranks win if two players have Two Pairs.

One Pair: Two cards of the same value, the others all singletons. Highest ranked pair or highest singleton wins.

High Card: Any hand which is not one of those listed above. Highest value wins. If there is a tie for highest, then the next highest wins, and so on.

Introducing Wild Cards, either by having a Joker, or naming the deuce (2) as wild, extends the range of possibilities. Five of a Kind now becomes top scorer, with four Aces plus the wild card beating any other combination.

Draw Poker

To choose the dealer, any player distributes cards from a shuffled pack: first to get a Jack becomes the first dealer. The cards are shuffled three times, lastly by the dealer, and the player to dealer's right cuts.

Cards are dealt one at a time, from the dealer's left, until each player has five cards.

Betting: Stakes should be agreed in advance (cash or chips). Each player places a chip in the pool at the start. One player acts as Banker. Betting normally starts to the dealer's left and goes clockwise. In some schools, no player is allowed to open the betting unless he holds a pair of Jacks or a higher combination. You can either call, raise or fold (sometimes called drop). If you fold, you discard your hand and lose your stake. If you call, you must put into the pool enough chips to match, but not exceed, what any other player has bet in that round. If you raise, you add more value to the call amount, subject to an agreed upper limit. When you raise, you must say clearly the amount you are raising by. Once everyone has made a bet, or folded, the players still in the game may discard up to three cards, and receive replacement cards from the dealer. Another betting round follows and the players again call, raise or fold. Previous bets cannot be withdrawn. At the end of each betting round, each player has to have put the same amount into the pool. Players who don't do this, must fold.

The Showdown: This is when hands are shown. The highest hand (see Scoring) wins the pot.

STUD POKER

Arrangements for ante-ing stakes and choosing dealer as for Draw Poker.

Five-Card Stud: The dealer deals a round of cards face-down (the "hole-card"), then a round of cards face-up. Each player looks at his own hole-card. The player with the highest upcard (nearest the dealer if there is a tie) either bets or folds. Other players in sequence from the left call, raise or fold. Another upcard is then dealt to each player still in the game, beginning with the player with the top pair of upcards, and the player with the three best upcards opens the betting. Finally, a fourth upcard is dealt, and the round of betting is done on the same basis as before. After the final call, all hole cards are turned over and each player's whole hand exposed.

Six-Card Stud: In this version there is an additional deal added at the end, of a second face-down hole-card. But only five cards are produced for the showdown, leaving the player to decide which card to eliminate.

WHISKEY POKER ★★

The players ante agreed and equal amounts into the pool. Dealer is chosen as for standard poker.

The dealer deals five cards to each player, with an extra Hand, the "widow" dealt face-down on the table. Eldest Hand starts play, and he may take up the widow and replace it with his own Hand, face-up, or refuse it. If he refuses, the choice passes to his left. If every player refuses the widow, then the dealer spreads it face-up on the table. Now, starting again with eldest Hand, a player can pick up the whole widow, or draw just one card from it, replacing it either with his own Hand or one card from his Hand, or stand (decline to draw). Once he has done so, or stood, the turn passes to his left, and so on until one player knocks on the table to signify he is happy with his Hand. The other players now have one more chance each, to draw or to stand. There are no bets or raises within the game, and it now goes straight to the showdown, in which each player shows his Hand. Scoring the Hands is as for standard poker, and the winner takes the pool.

PONTOON ***

Also known in the USA as Blackjack, and in France as Vingt et Un (Twenty-One)

The Aim: To form a Hand whose total value is twenty-one, or which beats the dealer's.

Number of Players: From two to eight or more.

Scoring Values: Ace can be 1 or 11 at the player's choice; Kings, Queens, Jacks and 10's are all ten; other cards are at their pip value.

The Method: Use the standard 52-card pack (two packs shuffled together for eight or more players). Cut for banker (highest card; he is also the dealer). The banker deals one card to each player, starting on his left and ending with himself. His card remains face down; everyone else picks up their card. Starting from the banker's left, the players place their initial bets (between agreed maximum and minimum levels). The banker then deals a second card to each player, and now all the players including the banker look at their two cards. If the banker has a Pontoon (Ace - at 11 - plus a 10), he lays it down, face-up. Each player has to pay double their stake to the banker, and the round ends.

If the banker cannot declare a Pontoon, then each player, starting from his left has an opportunity to acquire extra cards. A player with a Pontoon declares it at this point by placing it on the table, the 10 face down and the Ace face-up on top of it. A player with two cards of equal value can split, by laying them face-up on the table and placing another stake equal to his first one. The banker deals another card, face-down, to each of these. If again there are equal-value cards, there can be a further split. Each of these hands may then be played, one after the other, during the player's turn.

Note: If the split cards are 10-point ones, they must be of the same nominal rank; two Jacks may be split but a Jack and a king cannot.

If a player's cards total under twenty-one, he can say "I'll buy one". He must bet again by the same amount as before, or up to double it, but not more. The banker then deals him another card. If his total is still under twenty-one, he can buy again, once again increasing his stake. This time he can raise it by any amount between the first bet and the second. If the total is still under twenty-one, he can buy and bet again, in the same way. Instead of buying, if his total is under twenty-one, a player can say "Twist". This means no increase in the stake, and the banker deals him another card. The player can then Twist again if his total is low, until he has up to five cards in his hand. Five cards totalling under twenty-one form a Five Card Trick (see next page). A player can buy and then twist, but not twist and then buy. A player may decide to take no extra cards, and say "Stick". This is usual if his hand totals fifteen or more. Play then passes to the next player on the left. If at any time a player's hand exceeds twenty-one, he is "bust", and must throw in his hand, face-up, and lose his stake to the bank. A player who is bust on one split hand can still play the other. When the players have completed their turns, the banker turns his two cards face-up. He can then add up to three extra cards, or stay with his hand. At the end of the round, after scoring is completed, there are several possibilities: If no-one had a Pontoon, the dealer adds all the used cards to the bottom of the pack and deals again, without shuffling. If there was a Pontoon, the cards are shuffled and cut before the next deal. There is no change of banker unless he did not have a Pontoon, and another player did have one, without splitting his hand. That player then takes over the bank. If two or more players are eligible, then the one nearest the banker's left becomes the new banker. A banker can also sell the bank to another player, after any round.

MADE IN BELGIUM

49

Scoring and Paying: If the banker has over twenty-one, he is bust. He pays their stakes back to all players who have not also gone bust, with double to anyone with a Pontoon Or a Five Card Trick. If the banker has twenty-one or less, with not more than four cards, he pays their stake back to any player with a higher hand value, and collects from those with an equal or lower value. A banker who stayed on nineteen will say "Paying Twenty". All players then show their cards; those with twenty-one or a Five Card Trick receive double their stake. A banker with twenty-one pays on Pontoons and Five Card Tricks. If the banker has a Five Card Trick, he pays only Pontoons (double the stake). Every other player, even those with Five Card Tricks, pay double their stake to the banker.

RACING DEMON **

Number of Players: Two.

The Aim: To be first to get rid of your Demon pile, and to score 200 points.

The Method: Two 52-card packs are needed, with backs of different pattern or colour: one pack for each player. Aces are low. Each player deals thirteen cards face-down into a pile - these are the demon piles. The top card of each pile is turned over. Each player then deals a further four cards from his stock, placing them individually in a row to the right of the demon pile. These make the bases of foundation piles and can be built on in descending order of alternate colours (e.g. black 5, red 4, black 3, and so on). Cards can be added from the stock or from the turned-up top cards of the demon piles. Cards from the stock piles are turned up in sets of three: a card which cannot be used goes into a discard pile which becomes the stock once the original stock is exhausted. As Aces become available, they are placed face-up, separately, forming eight piles upon which either player can build in upwards sequence, treating the ace as low. Cards can be transferred to these piles but must then remain there. The aim is to get rid of the thirteen cards in your demon pile.

Scoring: The winner of a round scores 10. Each player scores one point for every card played (i. e. not in the demon pile, the stock or the discard pile). The player with cards left in his demon pile doubles their value and subtracts this from his total of played cards. If Kings are placed on the foundation piles, an extra ten points is awarded for each King.

RED DOG *

Number of Players: Three can play, but the game is best with more than four.

The Aim: To take a chance on having a higher card than the top card of the stock pile.

The Method: Each player puts an agreed amount of chips or cash into the pool. Use the standard 52-card pack. Cut for dealer (highest card). The dealer deals five cards to each player, or four if the number of players is nine or more. The remaining cards are placed face-down on the table, as the stock. The player to the dealer's left, having looked at his hand, bets anything from one chip to the whole pool that he holds a higher card of the same suit as the (unseen) top card on top of the stock. He must place his chips or coins alongside the pool. The dealer turns the top card over. If the player can produce a higher card of the same suit, then the dealer returns his stake and pays him from the pool. If the player loses, his bet goes into the pool and he shows his whole hand, face-up, after which it is discarded, and play passes to the next player on the left. A player can pass (not offer a bet) but must then pay one chip to the pool. If a player wins the whole pool, then each player contributes an equal amount to form a new pool and restart the game. If a player leaves the game, the pool must be equally divided and the game restarted.

RUMMY **

Number of Players: Two to six.

The Aim: To be the first player to "go out" by getting rid of all cards.

The Method: Use the standard 52-card pack. Aces are low. Cut for dealer (lowest card). Dealer deals cards according to the number of players: ten each to two players; seven each to three or four; six each to five or more. Cards are dealt out individually in rotation from the dealer's left. The rest of the pack is placed face down in the centre of the table, and the top card is turned face-up to start the discard pile. Having looked at his hand, the player on the dealer's left draws a card either from the top of the pack (unseen) or from the discard pile, and arranges his hand into melds of three or four, either by suit (consecutive, as 3-4-5-6), or by value (as three Kings). He places the melds, if any, face-down in front of him. Whether or not he lays down melds, he discards a single card face-up on the discard pile. This is the "upcard". The next player to the left does the same. He can also add cards to the melds already laid down ("laying off").

A player does not have to lay down his melds; he can retain them and hope to go out in a single turn.

This is to go rummy. The process continues round the players until one "goes out" by melding, laying off, or discarding his last card. If the whole pack is exhausted and no-one has gone out, the discard pile can be turned over, and the last upcard used to start a new discard pile.

Scoring: The player who goes out scores points for all the cards still held by his opponents: 10 for each court card, 1 for each Ace, others according to their pip value. A player who goes rummy gets double points. Rummy can be, and often is, played as a gambling game rather than for points.

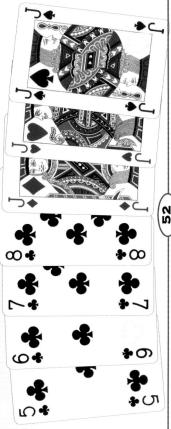

SERGEANT-MAJOR **

Number of Players: Three.

The Aim: To win the greatest number of tricks from a single hand.

The Method: Use the standard 52-card pack. Cut for dealer (highest card). The dealer deals 16 cards to each player. The last four cards are placed face-down, and form the kitty. The dealer chooses trumps. He then discards four of his cards, face-down, and picks up the kitty instead. The player to the dealer's left leads any card to the first trick. Other players must follow suit if they can, or trump, or discard. The trick is won by the highest card of the suit that led, or the highest trump. Each player has a target to meet. The dealer's is 8; the player's to his left is 5; the third player's is 3. At the end of the round, after scoring, the deal moves to the left. When the new deal is dealt, each player who was Up in the previous round gives away one card of his choice for each extra trick to a Down player, who must return the highest card he has of the same suit or suits. This can mean returning a card he has just been given. The game ends when any player wins 12 or more tricks from one hand.

Scoring: A player beating the target is said to Up by the difference between his score and the target; a player short of target is said to be Down by the same difference. Players who are Down pay one chip for each trick they are short by; players who are Up receive a chip for each extra trick.

SEVEN-UP **

Number of Players: Two to four, but two are best.

The Aim: To be first to reach seven points, by building up a trick-winning hand.

The Method: Use a standard 52-card pack. Aces are high. Draw for dealer - the higher card wins. Dealer deals six cards to each player, in two sets of three. The top card of the stock is then turned over to determine trumps. If a Jack is turned up, the dealer gets one point. The other player begins, by either standing (saying "I stand," and accepting the turned-up card as trumps) or begging (saying "I beg," and requesting a different suit). The dealer can accept or deny this request. If he accepts it, he deals three new cards to each and turns over the new top card of the stock, until a trump is agreed. If the dealer refuses to change trumps, the other player scores one point, and play continues. Each player, if necessary, discards enough cards to reduce his hand to six. The non-dealer leads, placing a card face-up. The dealer must follow suit, with a higher value, or play a trump to win the trick. Otherwise the trick goes to the other player. The winner of the trick leads the next card.

Scoring: Single points are won as follows:

High: The player dealt the highest trump in play

Low: The player dealt the lowest trump in play

Jack: The player winning the Jack of trumps in a trick (unless the dealer turned it over to determine trumps).

Game: The player with the highest total of point values for cards won in tricks. Values are: ace 4; King 3, Queen 2,Jack 1, ten 10. No other cards have any value. If only one trump card is played, it collects two points, or three if it is the Jack.

SKAT ***

Number of Players: Three.

The Aim: To be first to score ten game points.

The Method: Use a pack of 32 cards (Ace, King, Queen, Jack, 10, 9, 8, 7 in each suit). Cut for dealer (highest card). Dealer deals ten cards to each player, in sets of 3, then 4, then 3 at a time, and places the next two cards face-down on the table. These are the skat (also called the widow). The player to the dealer's left is First Hand. He has first right to pick up the skat. The player on his left (Middle Hand) is next if First Hand passes, and the third is Last Hand. He can pick up the skat if Middle Hand passes. The first player to take the skat is called the Player. He discards two cards face-down to replace the skat. First Hand leads (he may or may not be the Player). Others must follow suit if they can; if not, they may play any card. A trick is won by the highest card of the suit led, or by the highest trump. The winner of the trick leads to the next trick. If all three players pass, the aim of the games changes. Now it is to win as few points in tricks as possible. The skat is set aside, and First Hand leads in the normal way. The skat is added to the cards of the player who wins the last trick. This variation of the game the game is called Least.

Trumps and Point Values: All Queens and Jacks and all Diamonds are trumps. This does not change. Ranking order of trumps is as follows: Queens of Clubs, Spades, Hearts, Diamonds; then Jacks in the same sequence of suits. Then come the other Diamonds: Ace, 10, King, 9, 8, 7. In the other suits, the ranking is: Ace, 10, King, 9, 8, 7. Note that the 10 outranks the King. Point values: Ace 11; 10 10; King 4; Queen 3; Jack 2; others: nil.

Scoring: 1. If the skat has been taken up: If the Player takes from 61 to 90 points (see Point Values) he scores two Game Points. If he takes 91 or more points, he scores four Game Points (Schwarz). At the end of play, the point values of his two discards are also counted in his favour. If the Player falls short of his contract to win 61 or more points, he loses two Game Points if his score is between 31 and 60; and four Game Points (Schneider) if his score is under 31. If he takes no tricks at all, he loses six Game Points (Schwartz).

Scoring: 2. If the skat was not taken up: If a player has taken no tricks, he scores four Game Points. If a player has taken all the tricks, he loses four Game Points. If each player has taken at least one trick, the one with the lowest point value scores two Game Points. If two players tie with the same lowest point value, the two Game Points go to the player who lost the last trick between the two. If each player scores 40 value points, the dealer is awarded the two Game Points.

55

SOLO **

Number of Players: Four.

The Aim: The highest bidder plays against the other three to take the number of tricks he bid for.

The Method: Use a standard 52-card pack. Aces are high. Cut for dealer (highest card). The dealer deals 13 cards to each player, from his left, in batches of 3,3,3,3,1. The final card is turned up in front of the dealer to propose the trump suit. Bidding begins with eldest hand, and goes to the left. Players can make a higher bid, or pass, or accept a Proposal. A player who has passed once may not bid again, and if a bid is followed by three consecutive passes, the bidder is the Soloist. Possible bids, in ascending order, are:

Proposal: a player says "I propose," or "Prop", if he thinks he and a partner can take at least eight tricks using the proposed trump suit. If no bid follows, another player may accept this proposal by saying "I accept," or "Cop". If no further bid is made, this bid stands and the two play as partners for the round. A higher bid cancels the Proposal.

Solo: a bid to take at least five tricks using the proposed trump suit

Misere: a bid to take no tricks, playing at no trumps.

Abundance: a bid to win nine or more tricks using a trump suit named by the bidder.

Royal Abundance: a bid to win at least nine tricks using the proposed trump suit.

Spread Misere: a bid to win no tricks, playing at no trump, and with the hand placed face-up on the table after the first trick is played.

Abundance Declared: a bid to win all thirteen tricks, without a trump suit, but with the chance of leading to the first trick. This is the highest bid of all.

If eldest hand proposes and all others pass, he is able to raise his call to a Solo. If eldest hand passes, and another player proposes, without any higher call being made, eldest hand has the opportunity of accepting the proposal. If all pass, the cards are thrown in and the deal passes to the left. Once the contract is made, the dealer takes the turned-up card into his hand and eldest hand leads, except in the case of Abundance Declared (unless he is also the soloist). Tricks are taken in the normal way: players must follow suit if possible; and the winner of the trick leads to the next.

Scoring: If the soloist makes his contract, he receives points from the other players; otherwise he pays points:

Proposal and Acceptance: 2 points

Solo: 2 points

Misere: 3 points

Abundance (including Royal): 4 points

Spread Misere: 6 points

Abundance Declared: 8 points

In the case of Proposal/Acceptance, each of the partners receives or pays.

SPOIL FIVE ***

Number of Players: Two to ten.

The Aim: To win three or five tricks, or to stop the other players from doing so, leaving the pool un-taken.

The Method: Use a standard pack of 52 cards. Each player puts an agreed number of tokens or coins in the pool. One player deals until a Jack is dealt: the recipient of the Jack becomes dealer, reshuffles, and deals for the game. Hands of five are dealt, either 2 cards each and then 3, or vice versa. The top card of the stock is turned over to identify trumps. If it is an Ace, the dealer may immediately pick it up, and discard another card. If another player is holding the Ace of trumps, he passes a discard, face down, to the dealer, in exchange for the uncovered trump card. If the dealer holds the ace of trumps, he discards under the stock, on his turn, and picks up the turned-up trump.

Eldest hand makes the opening lead. Others must then follow suit or trump. If unable to follow suit, any card may be played but the trick will be lost. The trick is won by the highest card in the suit, or by the trump (higher card if trumps were led). The winner of the trick leads the next card. Reneging is possible: if a low trump is led, and the other player is holding the 5 or Jack of trumps, or the Ace of Hearts, he may retain these and play another card. But if a trump card higher than any of his is played, he must play the same suit. If no player wins three tricks, the game is "spoiled". The dealing switches to the next player on the left, more tokens go in the pool, and the game resumes.

If a player wins three tricks he wins the pool. If he takes the first three tricks in a row, he can either throw in his cards or say "Jink". This means he expects to win the two remaining tricks, and if he does so, the opponents pay him an extra token. If he fails, the pool stands and a new round begins.

Ranking structure in Spoil Five:

Whatever the trump suit, the Ace of Hearts is always the third-highest trump card.

Ranking of trumps otherwise starts with the 5 as highest card.

Hearts: 5,Jack,Ace,King,Queen, 10, 9, 8, 7,6, 4, 3, 2.

Diamonds: 5,Jack, Queen of Hearts,Ace, King, Queen,10, 9, 8, 7,6, 4, 3, 2.

Clubs and Spades: as with Diamonds.

In non-trump suits, the ranking is different for the red and black suits:

Hearts: Ace, King, Queen, Jack, 10, 9, 8, 7, 6, 5, 4, 3, 2.

Diamonds: As Hearts, but with Ace low.

Clubs and Spades: King, Queen, Jack, Ace, 2, 3, 4, 5, 6, 7, 8, 9, 10.

SWITCH ✻

Also played as Eights (see Note).

Number of Players: Two to eight.

The Aim: To be first to put down all your cards.

The Method: Use the standard 52-card pack, or two packs if there are six or more players. Cut for dealer (highest card). Dealer deals five cards to each player, one at a time, or seven cards if only two are playing. The remaining cards are placed face-down to form the stock, and the top card is turned up and placed alongside the stock, as the starter. If it is an Ace, replace it randomly in the stock pile and turn over the next card.

From the dealer's left, each player in turn plays a card on to the table, face-up, making a row from the starter card. Each card played must be of the same rank or the same suit as the previous one. Aces are wild, and a player playing an ace can call a new suit to follow. It is not obligatory to play a card, but any player who does not, or cannot, must carry on drawing cards from the stock until he plays one. The game ends when one player has played all his cards; or if no-one can play a further card.

Scoring: Each opponent awards the winner points or payment relating to the value of the cards he is left holding. Aces are 50 points, all court cards 10, other cards by their pip value. If the game ends in a block, all players count their hands, and the player with the lowest total collects from each opponent the difference between his score and theirs.

Note: This game can also be played as Eights, when the eights are wild. The rules are the same, but in scoring, Aces count for 1 point and eights for 50. See also the game of Crazy Eights.

WHIST **

Number of Players: Four, playing as two sets of partners.

The Aim: To take more tricks than the opposing partnership.

The Method: Use the standard pack of 52. Normally two packs are employed, with different back designs, so that one may be shuffled while the other is being dealt. Aces are high.

Players draw cards to decide partners, who sit facing each other across the table. The draw can be decided according to either suit or value. A draw is also made to find the dealer (highest card, with aces low).

The dealer deals out thirteen cards to each player, one at a time, starting with the player to his left. The last card is turned face-up to determine trumps: the dealer then adds it to his hand.

The player to the dealer's left leads to the first trick. Others must follow suit if they can, otherwise trump or discard. The highest card of the led suit or a trump card wins. One partner for each side takes charge of the side's won tricks. The winner of a trick leads to the next trick.

Scoring: A partnership, or pair, has to take at least seven tricks to score. The first six tricks won have no scoring value. After the seventh, each trick counts for one point. The first side to gain five points wins the game. Revoking is penalised by three points. The first side to gain five points wins the game. Points are also given for honour cards held. If a pair receive Ace, King, Queen and Jack of the trump suit (honour cards), they gain an extra four points. If they receive any three of the honour cards, they gain an extra two points. Points for honour cards are only given to a side which starts the deal with a score of less than four points.

Winning: Whist is normally played in a set of three games (a Rubber). The first side to win two games out of three wins the Rubber.

Note: The normal lead is the fourth card in your longest non-trump suit.

(60)

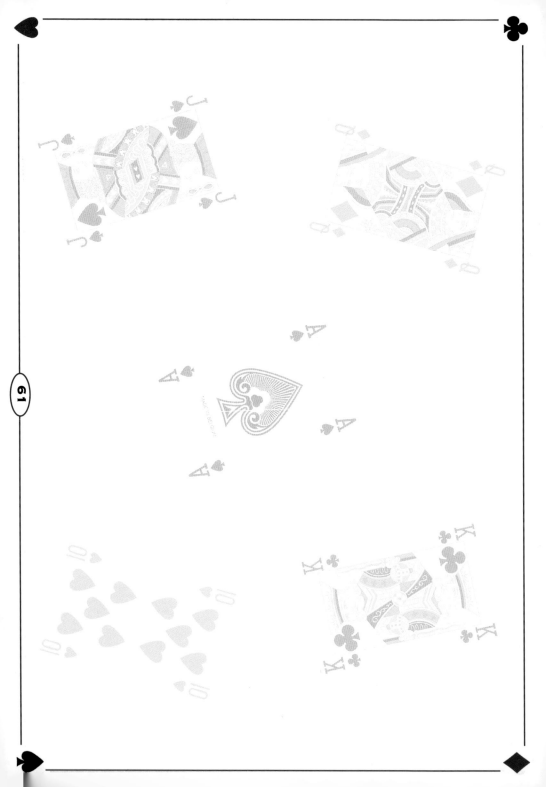